To root, to toot, to Parachute

What is a Verb?

To root, to toot, to Parachute

What is a Verb?

by Brian P. Cleary
illustrated by Jenya Prosmitsky

BOOK HOUSE

Take out the rubbish, or sharpen your knife –

Verbs are part of your everyday life.

To root,
to toot,
to parachute,

To play the saxophone or flute,

To dare,
defend,

descend,
disturb –

If it's an action,
it's a verb!

Verbs are words like sing and dance,

Pray or practise,

preach or prance,

Toss and tumble,
jump and jam,
Whine
and whisper,
sleep and slam.

So are yell,
help
and hold,

Whack and stack
and pack and fold,

Fix and finish,

load and lift,

Hurry, scurry shake and sift.

So take a present,

send your thanks,

Pull a tooth,
or pull some pranks,

BlOW a bubble,

sew a sleeve,

You'll use

a verb for each of these.

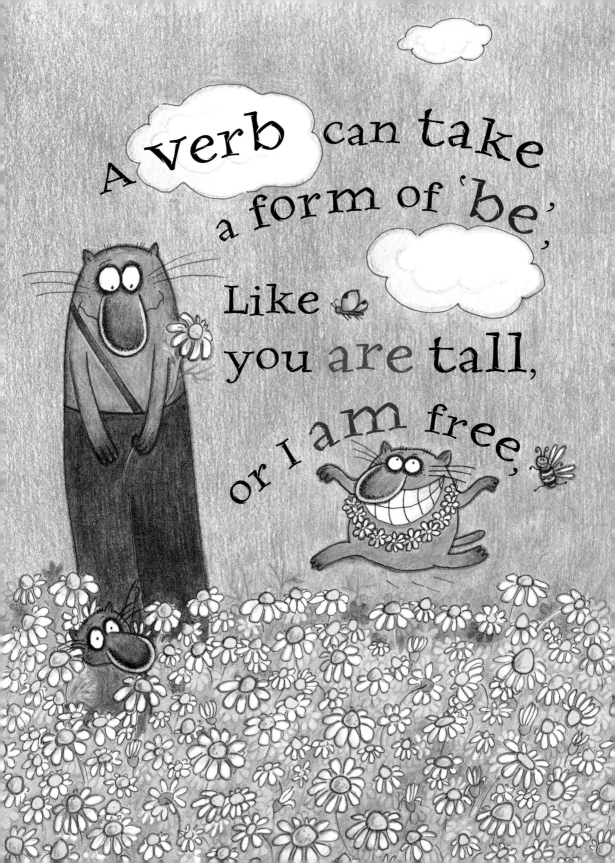

That is fun,

It's been great,

Were you the one who was so late?

Punt or pass or shoot or score,

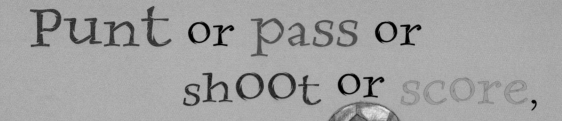

swim or paddle, float or pour,

Jog
or
juggle,

jig or leap,

Verbs can
leave you
in a heap.

Have and has
belong
here too,

Like "I have
green eyes,

she
has
blue."

"Jo has hair that curls a lot."

These verbs tell us who's got what!

Verbs tell of ships cruising, dogs snoozing, slime oozing,

They tell of spies spying, guys trying and losing,

Of leaves when they're falling and wind when it's blowing,

The rain when it's raining,

the snow when it's snowing.

They tell us of dogs
that are barking
or sleeping,

Of cars that are racing,
or merely
beep-beeping,

BEEP
BEEP

Of planes
that are
flying
and trains
choo-choo-chooing,
Aunt Edna
"Oh-Hi-ing"
and Mum
"Toodle
-ooing",

Whether
it's dangerous,
dull, or superb,
Each sentence, you see,
just must
have a verb!

VERBS ARE COOL

VERB POWER

AUTHOR: BRIAN P. CLEARY is the author of several other books for children, including *A mink, a fink, a skating rink: What is a Noun?*

ILLUSTRATOR: JENYA PROSMITSKY grew up and studied art in Kishinev, Moldova, and now lives in Minneapolis in the USA. Her two cats, Henry and Freddy, were vital to her illustrations for this book.

To Mary Kate, Jack and Colin — three 'action' kids — B.P.C.

To my sister, Margarita — J.P.

Published in Great Britain in 2003 by
Book House, an imprint of
The Salariya Book Company Ltd
25 Marlborough Place, Brighton BN1 1UB

Please visit the Salariya Book Company at:
www.salariya.com
www.book-house.co.uk

ISBN 1 904194 61 3

A catalogue record for this book is available from the British Library.

Printed and bound in USA.